Written by Kevin Pettman

Edited by Frances Evans

Cover Design by Angie Allison

Designed by Derrian Bradder
and Jelene Spencer

EAST AYRSHIRE LEISURE	
1314000606002 3	
Askews & Holts	
JB782.421	
BELLFIELD	

First published in Great Britain in 2020 by Buster Books, an imprint of
Michael O'Mara Books Limited, 9 Lion Yard, Tremadoc Road, London SW4 7NQ

W www.mombooks.com/buster   F Buster Books   🐦 @BusterBooks

Text copyright © Buster Books 2020
Artwork adapted from www.shutterstock.com

A CIP catalogue record for this book is available from the British Library.

ISBN: 978-1-78055-731-1
**PLEASE NOTE: This book is not affiliated with or endorsed
by Billie Eilish or any of her publishers or licensees.**

1 3 5 7 9 10 8 6 4 2

This book was printed in August 2020 by
Shenzhen Wing King Tong Paper Products Co. Ltd.,
Shenzhen, Guangdong, China.

Picture credits
Front cover: dpa picture alliance / Alamy Stock Photo
Back cover: Bryan Steffy / Stringer / Getty

Page 2–3: Axelle/Bauer-Griffin / Contributor / Getty; Page 7: Gareth Cattermole / Staff / Getty;
Page 9: Rich Fury / Staff / Getty; Page 14: Lorne Thomson / Contributor / Getty;
Page 17: Young Hollywood / Contributor / Getty; Page 19: Kevin Mazur / Contributor / Getty;
Page 20–21: Steven Ferdman / Contributor / Getty; Page 22: Rich Fury / Stringer / Getty;
Page 25: Tim Mosenfelder / Contributor / Getty; Page 27: Kevin Mazur / Contributor / Getty;
Page 28: Kevin Winter / Staff / Getty; Page 35: Neilson Barnard / Staff / Getty;
Page 37: Steve Granitz / Contributor / Getty; Page 39: Tim Mosenfelder / Contributor / Getty;
Page 45: Katja Ogrin / Contributor / Getty; Page 46: Jeff Kravitz / AMA2019 / Contributor / Getty;
Page 48: Jeff Kravitz / Contributor / Getty; Page 51: Paul Bergen / Contributor / Getty;
Page 52: Jon Kopaloff / Stringer / Getty; Page 61: Emma McIntyre / Staff / Getty;
Page 62–63: Michael Hickey / Contributor / Getty

BILLIE EILISH

Buster Books

CONTENTS

With her stunning voice, amazing musical talent and trendsetting style, Billie Eilish is an artist like no other. She shot to fame in her mid teens with breathtaking songs and videos. Billions of worldwide streams, sellout global tours, record-breaking achievements and awards, and her passionate fans and followers prove that Billie has rocked the music scene. Can you imagine being a pop-culture icon before you have even blown out the candles on your 18th birthday cake? Billie can.

Billie is known for being a deep, serious artist. She openly admits to having had problems with depression and her mental health and doesn't hide these issues in her lyrics, stage shows, videos and interviews. Her millions of supporters, who range from teenagers and young adults to older fans, admire her honesty and straight-talking style.

Get to know and understand Billie, though, and you will also see a very passionate artist and happy individual beneath the intense song lyrics. Billie thrives on realness; she lives with her parents in her childhood Los Angeles home, makes music in her bedroom and hangs out with friends who've known her since she was a kid. She loves writing and performing alongside her older brother, Finneas, and wearing the eye-catching clothes, jewellery and trainers that create her unique style. Billie is lucky that her talent for music has already given her a career that is financially and emotionally rewarding.

> **"I did not start writing music because I was like 'ooh, I'm gonna write music so that I can get famous'. I never really felt like that."**

Although she's not on a mission to change the world with her music, Billie appreciates that her pop platform gives her a chance to touch the lives and impact the wellbeing of her fans, as well as people from entirely different backgrounds. She's also not afraid to speak out on important topics such as feminism, the environment and the benefits of being a vegan.

Being perhaps the most recognized teenager on the planet comes with immense pressure. Billie is insanely famous and has a huge presence on social media, websites and in magazines. Despite this, fame has never been her driving force. "I did not start writing music because I was like 'ooh, I'm gonna write music so that I can get famous'. I never really felt like that," she told Beats 1 when she was 16.

So, turn the page to enter the mind-blowing world of Billie Eilish. Discover her amazing achievements in the entertainment world and the truth behind her powerful music, videos, style and beliefs.

NAME:
Billie Eilish

DATE OF BIRTH:
18th December, 2001

BIRTHPLACE:
Los Angeles

LIVES:
Los Angeles

FIRST HIT:
'Ocean Eyes'

FIRST STUDIO ALBUM:
When We All Fall Asleep, Where Do We Go?

GLOBAL STREAMS:
15 billion+

MUSIC STYLE:
Electro pop, indie pop, EDM, rock

"I THINK TRYING TO

LIMIT SOMETHING

AND PUT IT IN A

BOX IS SUCH A

SMALL THING TO DO."

Billie's music does not fall neatly into one category, and she dislikes the way some music has to be defined as one thing or another. In a chat with *Teen Vogue*, she revealed: "I don't like genres of music. I think trying to limit something and put it in a box is such a small thing to do. If you like it and you're making it, then just keep making it." Her musical style and influences are widespread and her material has an ever-changing vibe as it swings from electro and indie pop and rock to electronic dance music (EDM) and haunting ballads.

Billie is not afraid to talk about the range of bands and artists that she has connected with and enjoyed listening to growing up. There's no embarrassment when she admits to being a massive fan of Justin Bieber! Green Day, Linkin Park, Avril Lavigne, Lana Del Rey, My Chemical Romance, Frank Sinatra and even The Beatles have shaped her rich and eclectic taste over the years.

"Music has always been in my life and I've always sung. I've never not been singing!"

Billie speaking to Apple Music in 2017

Billie believes that lyrics are the most important part of a song. The Beatles, who first wowed the world back in the 1960s, are an example she often uses of a band whose words and tunes mix together perfectly.

There is intent and meaning behind every song she writes herself or with her brother, but equally Billie is not overly bothered about explaining what all of her songs mean and represent. It doesn't matter to Billie if a song means something for one fan but has a completely different meaning to another. She likes to leave her work open to interpretation.

Just as Billie's music tastes are unusual, so too was her breakthrough into the music industry. Instead of having a

"PEOPLE USED TO SHUSH ME BECAUSE I WOULD JUST SING AND SING AND SING AND SING AND SING."

Billie speaking to Apple Music in 2017

powerful record company promoting her and having songs played on radio stations to push her into the mainstream, it was the digital world that first spotted her. In 2015 she recorded 'Ocean Eyes' along with her brother and released it on the sharing platform Soundcloud. Intended only for her friends to hear and her dance teacher to use as a backing track, the song soon gained traction and took off around the globe. That said, although the digital age helped to establish Billie, people suspect she would always have been discovered one way or another.

Now with multiple Grammys, American Music Awards, record-breaking albums and Spotify and YouTube superstardom to her name, Billie's rise looks to have no limits. For fans, that's music to their ears.

DID YOU KNOW?

Billie sang The Beatles' song 'Yesterday' at the Oscars in 2020. Her brother, Finneas, played the piano during the emotional performance.

BILLIE BELIEVES

"I LUCKILY HAD MUSIC — IF I DIDN'T HAVE MUSIC EVERYTHING WOULD BE SO BAD. I JUST WANT MY MUSIC TO GET IN PEOPLE'S HEADS."

"I DO GO ON INSTAGRAM TO SEE ART. WHERE ELSE AM I GOING TO SEE IT? YEAH THERE ARE MUSEUMS, BUT THIS KIND OF ART ISN'T IN MUSEUMS."

"WHY WOULD YOU EAT AN ANIMAL WHEN YOU CAN EAT SOME CHIPS? IT DOESN'T MAKE SENSE TO ME."

"YOU DON'T HAVE TO BE IN LOVE TO WRITE A SONG ABOUT BEING IN LOVE, AND YOU DON'T HAVE TO HATE SOMEONE TO WRITE A SONG ABOUT HATING SOMEONE. IT'S JUST FUN TO PUT YOURSELF IN A POSITION WHERE YOU WOULD NOT BE OTHERWISE."

"THE FANS ARE LIKE MY BEST FRIENDS. I DON'T KNOW HOW TO PUT THAT LOVE INTO A SENTENCE."

AWESOME EILISH INFO

She enjoys driving in LA and her first vehicle was a Dodge Challenger muscle car that she called 'the Dragon'.

Billie loves to dye her hair and she first coloured it purple when she was nine years old.

Billie can play the piano, guitar and ukulele.

Billie once became so involved in her live performances that she sprained her ankle while jumping to 'Bad Guy' on stage in Milan. She's worn a medical boot several times because of this injury.

In 2020, she created a fashion range with the clothing company H&M that uses sustainably sourced, vegan-friendly materials. The range included a printed sweatshirt dress, waist bag and bucket hat.

Billie was born and raised in Los Angeles but she doesn't like the warm weather in California. In fact, she hates the LA sunshine!

Billie's name is an interesting story in itself. Born on 18th December, 2001 in California, her full name is actually the memorable mouthful of Billie Eilish Pirate Baird O'Connell. Wow!

Her parents are Maggie Baird and Patrick O'Connell, who themselves are musical and involved in acting, theatre and dance. 'Pirate' was going to be Billie's only middle name, but then her uncle suggested that it had a negative meaning, so she ended up with a very long official name. She chooses to be known as just Billie Eilish, but her brother goes by Finneas O'Connell.

As a young child heavily influenced by her adoring and free-spirited parents, Billie was always creative and active. She loved to dance around her house and in the garden, and enjoyed dance classes and putting on performances. Billie also got involved with gymnastics from a young age, which was another way of expressing herself that she excelled at. A quick YouTube search reveals a video of the youngster performing an aerial gymnastics routine, dangling and twisting from a silk rope. The display shows just how talented she was in many areas, even at a young age.

"I was just a kid who had a lot of time to focus on things that I wanted to focus on."

Billie speaking to Apple Music in 2017

When Billie was about ten, all of a sudden she developed a passion for horses and horse riding. Entranced by the graceful creatures, she begged her parents to allow her to ride, but her loving mum and dad could not afford lessons. Billie understood this but, as a sign of the hard work and determination she would eventually show in her singing career, she helped out at the horse stables all day for two summers. In exchange, she was able to ride the horses. This showed that if Billie had a dream or a goal, she would fight for it.

IF BILLIE HAD A DREAM OR A GOAL, SHE WOULD FIGHT FOR IT.

In her music career, Billie is heavily involved in the direction and style of her song videos, and this was perhaps sparked by her interest in filming as a little girl. At home, Billie would set up a digital camera and basic video equipment in the garden to take pictures and record fun moments. Sometimes, she would simply capture stones and blades of glass in an artistic way. She also arranged her toy animals as part of the recording. How cute!

Among her varied passions and energetic pastimes growing up, singing remained Billie's number-one fascination. The family sang together all the time. As Billie's mother is also a skilled songwriter and has conducted songwriting classes, it was perhaps inevitable that Billie and her brother would start composing their own lyrics and tunes.

DID YOU KNOW?

When Billie was on tour in Auckland, New Zealand in 2019, she caught some downtime by going horse riding along a local beach.

A big part of Billie's creative and artistic passion comes from the freedom she had as a child. She never went to school (well, she did — just not like most other children do!). Billie and Finneas were homeschooled, which meant that Maggie and Patrick taught them at home instead of sending them to a regular school. You might think this meant that Billie was lonely and missed having school friends around. In fact, the singer looks back fondly at the time she spent at home, learning about topics that interested her and would help her in later life.

"I've never been to school. I never was at school so never had to quit school. The things I need to do in my life don't have to do with science and math."
Billie in an interview with KROQ-FM in 2018

Speaking in 2018, Billie's mum said she never regrets having Billie and Finneas homeschooled. "It just allowed them to have this creative life. The currency of the family was music and dance and creativity and comedy." This unusual situation did not stop Billie having some traditional school experiences. "At six years old, she told us she wanted to sing in a talent show," her mum said. Billie can still remember attending talent shows with other homeschooled children, and how fun and crazy it was.

When Billie was eight years old, she took another major step on her journey to success. Following in the footsteps of her brother, she became part of the Los Angeles Children's Chorus (LACC), which is a famous choir that helps children develop their singing talent. "I joined the choir when I was eight, mainly because my brother was in it and I thought that was really cool," Billie explained. "To be in a room full of people who love singing as much as I do was really eye-opening."

"I JOINED THE CHOIR WHEN I WAS EIGHT, MAINLY BECAUSE MY BROTHER WAS IN IT AND I THOUGHT THAT WAS REALLY COOL."

So, by learning the art of songwriting from her mother, playing instruments and singing with her father, penning lyrics with her brother and receiving quality vocal training at LACC, it seemed obvious that Billie's later life would focus on music.

She says she wrote her first 'real song' aged about 12 in one of her mum's classes and has never looked back, but without her family's love and direction she perhaps never would have come to the world's attention.

DID YOU KNOW?

Billie is a huge Justin Bieber fan. When she was younger, her bedroom was covered in posters of the pop star.

The video for Billie's 2019 hit single 'Everything I Wanted' starts with a simple but striking message. Set against a minimal soundtrack and with a plain background, two sentences displayed on the screen sum up the relationship she has with the most important person in her life. They read: "Finneas is my brother and my best friend. No matter the circumstance, we always have and always will be there for each other."

Finneas is four years older than Billie and is a talented musician, songwriter and producer in his own right. He has been playing in bands since his teens and is a master at the keyboard, guitar and at creating music digitally.

Despite being less well known than Billie, Finneas does not compete with his sister for fame and success – the pair work together most of the time and support each other fully. Finneas admitted directly to his little sister at the Variety Hitmakers awards in 2019: "Just being Billie Eilish's brother is all I ever want to be. I love Billie more than anything else and I'm so grateful to you and I love you."

"I feel so incredibly lucky to get to work with her and spend as much time as we get to spend together working and travelling and writing and recording and playing shows. It's just a dream."

Finneas speaking to Apple Music in 2018

From their days together in the LACC choir and experimenting with music in their bedrooms, Billie and Finneas are now one of the best musical double acts of the 21st century. The first song they wrote together was 'Bellyache', which the pair released in 2017 with Finneas credited as the producer. They still write and record songs in their bedrooms at Mum and Dad's, preferring to stay away from studios and keep control over their output.

After the song and video for 'Bury A Friend' – which the duo admitted was quite weird and unusual even for them – came out in 2019, Finneas realized they could pretty much write, release and perform whatever they liked. The music industry had no power to tell them what to do, as what they did together just felt so right. 'Bury A Friend' was actually written and recorded by Finneas and Billie in only one day, which just happened to be Finneas' 21st birthday. Happy birthday, big bro!

NAME:
Finneas Baird O'Connell

DATE OF BIRTH:
30th July, 1997

BIRTHPLACE:
Los Angeles

LIVES:
Los Angeles

INSTRUMENTS:
Guitar, bass, piano, keyboard

MUSICAL SKILLS:
Writing, singing, producing

DID YOU KNOW?

Finneas appeared on TV in the popular high-school singing show *Glee* when he was a teenager.

ACCOUNTS TO FOLLOW

WEBSITE
billieeilish.com
Billie's official website, covering music releases and news, merch at her official store and social media links.

TWITTER
@billieeilish
The official Twitter account for Billie, revealing clips, news and promotions.

YOUTUBE
BILLIE EILISH
All of Billie's released videos and albums.

INSTAGRAM
@billieeilish
Get an in-depth look at the exciting world of the young star. Browse Billie's posted videos, official announcements and teasers.

FACEBOOK
@billieeilish
The official account for connecting and sharing with the artist and other Billie Eilish fans.

SOUNDCLOUD
BILLIE EILISH
The platform that originally catapulted Billie to stardom.

November 2015 is a memorable month for Billie. It was then that, one evening, Billie and her brother first uploaded the song 'Ocean Eyes' to the streaming platform Soundcloud. It set her on the road to becoming a music superstar and the world's hottest young artist.

> "Soundcloud is like the GOAT [Greatest Of All Time]. Soundcloud is the only reason I am anything. 100%. We are in a time where anyone can make music which is so dope and Soundcloud is the only reason we can all do this."

Billie speaking to the OMR Podcast in 2019

Billie and Finneas had written songs together before, but 'Ocean Eyes' was the track that alerted the world to Billie's amazing talent. It was actually written by Finneas for his band, but when Billie was asked by her dance teacher to create a song that would that would work well with a choreographed dance, the pair thought about 'Ocean Eyes'. At first they were just going to send Billie's recording to her teacher, but then they decided to share it on Soundcloud. The siblings had no idea how huge it would become.

Billie was amazed that 'Ocean Eyes' gained over 1,000 plays within the first couple of days. At first she thought one of her popular friends had posted it, helping it to get some notoriety, but when the music website Hillydilly.com began creating a buzz around the hot new song, the numbers for 'Ocean Eyes' just grew and grew. Remember that Billie was still only 13 at the time!

A couple of years later, Billie spoke about how the lyrics of 'Ocean Eyes' reflected the mood she was in when she recorded it. "I was really into this boy, with this curly brown hair and these deep blue eyes. Whenever I looked at him I just got lost in his ocean eyes." It's clear that the words, created independently by her brother, struck a chord with Billie. "Can't stop staring at those Ocean Eyes," is how the opening line ends. "Burning cities and napalm skies" are lyrics that hit a much deeper feeling, as Billie describes her agonizing emotions.

When the chorus begins, "No fair" is sung beautifully by Billie in a long and powerful way. This mix of petulant language plays on teenage angst and gives the song a wonderfully catchy combination of short words and meaningful sentences. "When you realize you're falling in love with someone it can be scary. Even though I'm really young, I've gone through stuff like that and you're not in control," she revealed in an interview.

By April 2020, the official video for the song from 2016 had clocked up over 250 million YouTube hits. "'Ocean Eyes' specifically is what made me get where I am. I could never be more grateful than that. I'm really happy with what it's done," Billie said.

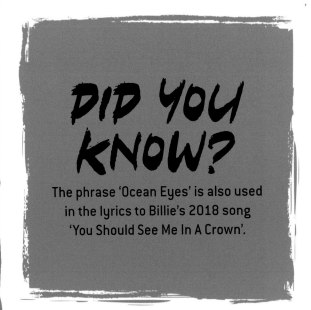

DID YOU KNOW?

The phrase 'Ocean Eyes' is also used in the lyrics to Billie's 2018 song 'You Should See Me In A Crown'.

The anticipation around Billie's first studio album, which finally dropped in 2019, was incredible. The teenager had been racking up millions of hits and downloads for a few years, thanks to singles such as 'Ocean Eyes', 'Bored', 'Copycat' and 'Six Feet Under', and sellout shows and concerts.

Signed to Darkroom/Interscope Records, her debut EP (extended play record) was a taste of what was to come. Called *Don't Smile At Me*, and released in summer 2017, the EP's nine songs represented Billie's varied style and her individual talent. One music writer described it as "dreamy and depressing, enchanting and haunting." The excitement around her full studio album was off the chart.

In spring 2019, *When We All Fall Asleep, Where Do We Go?* stunned the music world. The album shot straight to number one in the UK Official Chart and spent three weeks in the slot, making Billie the youngest female artist to secure a number-one album in the chart's history. In the US Billboard 200, it also debuted at the top spot and just six months later was a double platinum album, meaning two million units had been sold. On Spotify, the figures were equally impressive; it was the most streamed album of 2019 (something never achieved by a female artist before) and Billie's total streams clocked over six billion.

So what's the story and inspiration behind this chart-busting album? Finneas admitted to *Rolling Stone* that the album took around a year and a half to create because he and Billie were so keen to get it right. Initially, he and his sister thought it could be done in a matter of weeks. Fortunately, there was no pressure from the record label to get Billie's first album out there – instead, the label allowed her popularity to steadily grow and for the teenager to become comfortable with her music and career path. Speaking to *Vanity Fair* in October 2018, Billie said she was keen to finish the album, though, and six months after its release the following

ONE MUSIC WRITER DESCRIBED IT AS "DREAMY AND DEPRESSING, ENCHANTING AND HAUNTING."

year, she revealed even more about the lengthy process involved. "Exhausting! Me and Finneas have had conversations when we were like, 'Can you believe we actually finished the album?' We thought we would never finish."

When We All Fall Asleep, Where Do We Go? is clearly a huge achievement that Billie is very proud of. Every song and every sentence means something to her. "I love that album!" she quickly added after describing the time it took to create it. "It's a feeling I have never really felt. It's kind of a beautiful, relieving, excited, nervous, horrible, want-to-throw-up-type feeling," she went on to explain. "It's kinda been perfect ... a little bit!"

DID YOU KNOW?

"When we all fall asleep, where do we go?" is a lyric from 'Bury A Friend', which is one of the songs on the album.

When asked how she would recommend her fans listen to *When We All Fall Asleep, Where Do We Go?*, Billie gave an interesting response. "Listen in your car, either alone or with your best friend or someone who can understand how much you love the things that you love," she said with a wry smile. You get the impression that her fans were never far from her mind when she created the album. At the same time, it's clear that Billie wanted to convey her own deep thoughts and beliefs in each song. The album is intense, with zero fluff and no pointless songs to just fill up the minutes.

'Bad Guy' (see page 29) is the most famous song from the album, with over 1.2 billion Spotify streams inside the first 12 months. But rather than have one runaway success and a sprinkling of minor songs, *When We All Fall Asleep, Where Do We Go?* is packed with tunes whose downloads number into the hundreds of millions. By early 2020, 'When The Party's Over' had registered over 791 million Spotify streams, while YouTube hits such as 'All The Good Girls Go To Hell' (133 million views) and 'You Should See Me In A Crown' (186 million views) prove that fans are absorbing the full range of Billie's output. She never wanted to be a one-hit wonder and the album's figures show that she definitely isn't.

"Everything is connected to something else. That's what is kind of interesting about the album."

Popular videos have helped to keep Billie in the spotlight as much as her songs have. 'Xanny', the second song on the album, has a video exploring the pain and torment of substance abuse, while 'Bury A Friend' shows Billie being pushed and pulled by mysterious gloved hands along with other horror-inspired motifs. Billie's visual interpretations of the album's songs cause as much debate as the lyrics do. Talking about the album's videos to Amazon Music, Billie explained that she has synesthesia, which is a condition where her senses are interconnected. This will often lead to her trying to link her feelings of touch, sense and smell together: "Everything is connected to something else. That's what is kind of interesting about the album."

All of the album's songs were recorded either in her brother's bedroom or in Billie's own room, using a microphone dropped in front of her as she relaxed on the bed. From bedroom dreams to chart-topping triumph, *When We All Fall Asleep, Where Do We Go?* deserves to hold a place alongside any other legendary album. Billie admits she feels pressure around her second album, but even if that takes another three years to make, the wait will be worth it.

DID YOU KNOW?

Billie says the album is based around the thoughts and feelings she has when she's asleep or trying to sleep. She has suffered a lot from sleep-related problems.

"LISTEN IN YOUR CAR, EITHER ALONE OR WITH YOUR BEST FRIEND OR SOMEONE WHO CAN UNDERSTAND HOW MUCH **YOU LOVE** THE THINGS THAT YOU LOVE."

As the second most-streamed Spotify song of 2019, 'Bad Guy' is one of Billie's most acclaimed pieces of work. The catchy and quirky tune, with a kicking bass line and dance-pop buzz, won two Grammy Awards in January 2020 and helped to keep her album at number one on both sides of the Atlantic. "It's been pretty surreal to have a song that just explodes, because I've never had that," Billie reflected at the end of 2019, after 'Bad Guy' had won her an army of new fans.

Billie and Finneas had always wanted the song to be the opening track on the album because it was such a powerful but playful anthem. The basic idea behind the lyrics is about people pretending to be something they're not – acting like they're tough and in control, when actually they're fake and pretentious. "It's basically making fun of everyone and their personas of themselves. Even mine," explained Billie in an interview with LA radio station KIIS-FM. "I'm that bad type, make-your-mama-sad-type," goes part of the tongue-in-cheek first chorus.

Both Billie and Finneas weren't sure that the song would be even a minor hit, let alone one of the most culturally iconic recordings of the 21st century. 'Bad Guy' plays around with the usual structure of writing pop songs, and the pair didn't think the song had a catchy riff or 'hook' to draw people in. As it turned out, the mix of the lyrics, lazy-sounding humming and random recordings used on the track proved to be something people couldn't get out of their heads.

"No girl has ever been like, 'I'm the bad guy!'"

Billie in an interview with *Variety* in 2019

Billie was also keen to experiment with the tone and speed of the track's ending, having been inspired by the songs 'Never' by J.I.D and 'Stuck In The Mud' by Isaiah Rashad. Both songs seem to stop in the middle and begin new songs towards the end. Compared to the punchy start, the final 40 seconds of 'Bad Guy' are much

THE BASIC IDEA BEHIND THE LYRICS IS ABOUT PEOPLE PRETENDING TO BE SOMETHING THEY'RE NOT.

slower and dispirited. This atmosphere is reinforced through the video, as Billie sits on top of a man while he slowly does press-ups. Before this, the video flits between Billie mocking 'bad guys' and asserting her own authority in fun ways, such as riding toddler bikes and wearing a snorkel as she pokes water-filled bags containing male heads.

Speaking to *Rolling Stone*, Billie joked that the song took a long time to come together – parts of it sat on their recording equipment for a year. Billie confessed that she and Finneas "had like 800 different versions" of the harmonies, and they took days to decide which one to go with. While the song took a lot of hard work, the process remained upbeat. "The song was one of the most fun songs to make, ever," she asserts.

DID YOU KNOW?

Billie recorded 34 different versions of the word "duh" in 'Bad Guy' until she and Finneas were happy with it.

MUSIC TO REMEMBER

Billie's hit list is already a long one, despite her only turning 18 in December 2019. From her debut 'Ocean Eyes' to the seminal 'Bad Guy', there are stacks of songs that show off her musical genius. She has a distinct sound and isn't afraid to experiment – the emotionally charged 'When The Party's Over', for example, doesn't have the toe-tapping guitar sounds and base of 'Bellyache'. Both songs, though, are unmistakably Billie.

BELLYACHE (2017)

This song explores feelings of guilt, which Billie says causes a "bellyache" inside her. Finneas had always wanted to create a song called 'Bellyache', but just needed to put it into context. The pair were in their garage at home playing around with melodies and guitar riffs when they penned it, and Billie developed part of the opening line. "My friends aren't far / In the back of my car / Lay their bodies," she sings. It's a sinister line about killing her friends, but it's an example of the character-style writing the siblings often adopt.

BILLIE'S INSPIRATION CAN COME FROM ANYWHERE.

YOU SHOULD SEE ME IN A CROWN (2018)

Billie's inspiration can come from anywhere. She and Finneas were watching the BBC's TV show *Sherlock* and heard a villainous character say, "You should see me in a crown." They both thought the sentence was so cool that they decided to write a song with that line as the central theme. It's slow, dark and eerie, with critics acclaiming it as a "sinister nursery rhyme" and a "brooding pop anthem". Billie's favourite line from the track is "I like the way they all scream" – even though it freaks her out a little!

BURY A FRIEND (2019)

The second song that Billie and Finneas penned about death and murder (after 'Bellyache'), this tune is as iconic for its sound as for the dark video that goes with it. As she told MTV, 'Bury A Friend' is written from the viewpoint of a monster under the bed, singing to the person lying on top. "Why aren't you scared of me? Why do you care for me?" Billie sings during the first 20 seconds. In the MTV interview, she explains: "It's not like I'm the monster because I'm your enemy. I feel like it can be out of love or it can be out of hate or it can be out of terror or fear or whatever. If you love someone too much, it can be more dangerous for you than to hate someone."

EVERYTHING I WANTED (2019)

In this track, Billie continues the night-time theme associated with her debut album. 'Everything I Wanted' recounts a nightmare she had about dying and nobody caring. Clearly an incident that shook her, the only person she could talk to about the experience was her brother. Her love for Finneas becomes the song's underlying theme. The accompanying piano and soft beats back up an emotional recording. "It might have been a nightmare, to anyone who might care," she sings softly early on. The song carries a deep significance for her, but Billie also wants fans to explore their own interpretations of it.

NO TIME TO DIE (2020)

Billie and Finneas were delighted to be asked to create a theme tune for the 25th installment in the iconic James Bond film series. This was her first single of 2020, gave Billie her first UK number one and led to a poignant performance at The Brits in London in February. A moving ballad, threaded with Finneas' piano playing and a supporting orchestra, 'No Time To Die' is both classic Billie and classic Bond, which is not an easy achievement. Unlike most of the hits by Billie and Finneas, this song was actually written and recorded on a tour bus in Texas after the duo felt uninspired while in the studio working on the track.

DID YOU KNOW?

The opening sound on 'You Should See Me In A Crown' is of knives sharpening. That is actually a recording of Billie's dad sharpening a knife in their kitchen at home!

RECORD-BREAKING BILLIE

In 2019, Billie was the second most-streamed Spotify artist — and the top-ranking female artist — around the world with over six billion streams.

The Los Angeles singer is also the youngest-ever female solo act to head the UK album chart. *When We All Fall Asleep, Where Do We Go?* reached number one when Billie was aged 17 years, three months and 18 days old.

In the USA, 'Bad Guy' was streamed nearly three million times on the first day of its release.

Billie is the first woman to have 14 songs on the US's Billboard Hot 100 chart all at the same time, after her first album dropped in spring 2019.

Billie scooped her first Brit Award in 2020 when she was given the prize for International Female Solo Artist, ahead of the likes of Ariana Grande and Camila Cabello.

She is the first person to win all four of the major Grammy awards in one year since 1981.

In January 2020, the 18-year-old became the youngest person to win the prestigious Album of the Year prize at the Grammy Awards. In total, she won five Grammys that year — Album of the Year, Record of the Year, Song of the Year, Best Pop Vocal Album and Best New Artist.

Billie is the first artist born in the 2000s to have a number-one single in the UK and the US. 'Bad Guy' was her first chart-topper in the States, and 'No Time To Die' was number one in Britain.

Billie has rocked MTV Awards all over the world. At the VMAs and EMAs in 2019, she was given the Best New Act trophy.

Watching Billie performing on stage, attending award ceremonies or creating fun YouTube videos, her unique visual style is clear. Her appearance is almost as impactful as her singing and music. 'Brand Billie' is the complete music and fashion package – and her style is something she cares passionately about.

CLOTHES

In an interview with *Vogue Australia*, Billie expanded on her views on dressing and clothes. "I want layers and layers and layers, and I want to be mysterious," she said. Fashion continues to be her "security blanket" and the way to express herself without having to say a word or act in a certain way. She has spoken out about how men are not judged for wearing baggy clothing, while she has to justify and explain her choices all the time. "Fashion is its own language and I use mine all day, every day."

"What I like about dressing like I'm 800 sizes bigger than I am is it kind of gives nobody the opportunity to judge what your body looks like."

Billie in an interview with *Vogue Australia* in 2019

HAIR

Blue, purple, silver, green, black, pink – it seems that Billie has had every hair colour in the rainbow! Her choices draw lots of attention and Billie has fun playing around with different looks. The 'Ocean Eyes' and 'Bellyache' videos saw her carry off a silvery, slightly lilac style. In contrast, at the Grammys and for the release of 'No Time To Die' she had switched to black with a green top. This style was even mimicked by her pop-star friend Demi Lovato.

SHOES

Billie's devoted to footwear and, in particular, trainers. She says that one of her favourite shoes is the retro Air Jordan XV, which is inspired by the X-15 fighter jet and was first released over 20 years ago. Speaking on the cultural YouTube channel Complex about how she likes to customize her trainers, Billie stated: "I like the idea of having something that nobody else has." As a child with little money, Billie looked for shoes in secondhand stores and loved discovering cool trainers that suited her individual style.

JEWELLERY

It's quite common to catch Billie wearing multiple rings on each finger, ten or more necklaces, dagger-like earrings and lots of wristwatches. Her liking for spectacular jewellery follows no set pattern but she obviously wants to make a statement. Blinging up like Billie takes some serious cash, though, and some of the Chanel chains, bracelets and chokers she's been spotted wearing have price tags well into four figures. Ker-ching!

ACCESSORIES

Hats, caps, bandanas, beanies, sunnies and even long fingernail extensions all make regular appearances as part of Billie's extended wardrobe. While, for practicality's sake, she tones this down for her energetic live shows, in interviews and photoshoots she'll add extravagant extras to boost her look. On Instagram, Billie often wears a balaclava or a mask to crank up the mystery and deliberate craziness of her style.

DID YOU KNOW?

Billie says one of the first big fashion items she remembers buying was a bright-yellow Tommy Hilfiger puffer jacket.

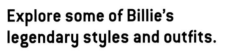

ICONIC OUTFITS

Explore some of Billie's legendary styles and outfits.

FESTIVAL FASHION

At the 2019 Coachella Valley Music and Arts Festival, Billie grabbed headlines with an outfit that was typical of her flamboyant fashion sense. A baggy, lime-green shirt and shoes were matched with blocky futuristic shades and a dark-patterned Louis Vuitton gilet over the top. The real crowd-stopper were her trousers, which were navy and a mix of fluffy and stretchy material. Billie only wore this outfit backstage, which was a shame for the thousands of fans out front.

BURBERRY BILLIE

Billie loves Burberry, the lavishly expensive British label with a distinctive plaid pattern on beige and light-brown garments. At the end of 2019 and into early 2020, the teenager wore baggy Burberry gear to both the American Music Awards and The Brits. Her outfit in London especially appeared a little more upmarket and reserved when compared to her usual street wear. She even went for Burberry designs on her fingernails!

BACK TO BLACK

When Billie turned up at the iHeartRadio Music Awards in an understated black outfit, the cameras went crazy. She matched a simple black, cargo-like jacket with black shorts and chunky black, silver-laced trainers. The showiest part was the design on her top and shorts. It was of the female hero Usagi Tsukino, from the Japanese manga series *Sailor Moon*.

GUCCI GIRL

Italian fashion house Gucci decked Billie out from top to toe at another LA arts event in 2019. The luxurious label crafted a blue, baggy, silky shirt and pants with a flowing silver pattern and golden-green embroidered flowers on the sleeves and legs. Styling it out with thick Gucci shades, Billie looked chic and classy while still achieving her comfy, non-conforming aura.

TREE-MENDOUS

How many world-famous teenagers would choose to wear a camo-like pattern of trees and flowers, let alone make it look ultra cool? Well, Billie did at the Variety Hitmakers ceremony and won much praise. Her over-sized cream coat with brown and beige floral features may have looked more like an old pair of curtains, but somehow she made it look totally awesome!

DID YOU KNOW?

Billie always wears shorts when performing on stage and never long trousers. Her shorts are baggy and come down past her knees.

Billie has always said that she would love to design a fashion collection of her own in the future. Her official website sells simple tops and beanie hats, plus chunky necklaces. All this gear carries her official logo, called 'Blohsh', which depicts a lopsided, gender-neutral figure. Blohsh even has its own Instagram account, with over 1.6 million followers within two years of its launch. When Billie expands her clothing business in the years ahead, she may well use this emblem.

Billie's obsession with her style, and the source of her individualism and trend setting, goes back to when she was a child. Billie's family was not wealthy and she would often make her own shirts and trousers, patching material together to create a look that suited her. She also experimented with cutting up shoes and mashing styles together in order to create a particular design that she had in mind. While laughing off her "janky" appearance back then, she's also proud that she had the spirit and determination to express herself and feel happy with how she dressed.

"I just like dressing out of my comfort zone. I want to dress in a way that if I was in a room full of people wearing regular clothes, I would be like, 'Oh, I bet everyone's looking at me.'"

Billie often describes her look as "wonky", meaning that stuff is oversized, out of balance and gives people plenty to think about when they see it. In a Beats 1 interview aged 15, she wore red shoes with inflatable pads strapped to them and proudly lifted them high for the camera to spot. At the same young age, Billie opened up to *Harper's Bazaar* about her image and why she likes dressing the way she does. "I just like dressing out of my comfort zone. I want to dress in a way that if I was in a room full of people wearing regular

"I WANT TO DESIGN A CAR; I WANT TO MAKE A MOVIE; I WANT TO HAVE A CLOTHING BRAND. THE ONLY THING THAT DOESN'T CHANGE ABOUT ME IS THE FACT THAT I'M GONNA CHANGE OVER AND OVER AGAIN."

Billie speaking in a Vevo LIFT interview in 2018

clothes, I would be like, 'Oh, I bet everyone's looking at me.' I want to feel that way. That's my casual."

Billie chooses to wear baggy gear because she feels comfortable in it and doesn't want to have her body shape discussed online. At the same time, it seems she wants to provoke a response and debate through her style: "I love being judged. I'm here for it." She also got involved with a campaign by famous US clothes company Calvin Klein called 'I Speak My Truth'. In the 30-second video, she wears a green tracksuit and is seen kissing a mirror as a sign of her inner happiness. "I never want the world to know everything about me. That's why I wear big, baggy clothes. Nobody can have an opinion because they haven't seen what's underneath, you know?" she revealed candidly.

BILLIE'S WELLBEING

"IT SHOULDN'T MAKE YOU FEEL WEAK TO ASK ANYONE FOR HELP, AND YOU SHOULD BE ABLE TO ASK ANYONE FOR HELP. EVERYONE HAS TO HELP SOMEONE IF THEY NEED IT."

Billie is open about her struggles with depression, and wants her fans to know that it's okay, and natural, to feel different thoughts. Being a teenager can be difficult and even before she became a global icon, Billie was battling with her mental health and trying to keep a positive state of mind.

Billie doesn't talk to the media about the experiences that have caused her to feel depressed at times, which is absolutely her choice. However, if asked to help with a mental health campaign or to talk about the ways young people can access support, she is only too happy to get involved. In a revealing chat with the Ad Council's YouTube channel, she talks about how people have texted her supportive messages just at the moment that she needed to feel loved, and how asking for help and talking to friends and trained professionals is a great step to take. "It shouldn't make you feel weak to ask anyone for help, and you should be able to ask anyone for help. Everyone has to help someone if they need it."

When Billie was feeling at her lowest and having her darkest thoughts, she admits that the support she had from her mum was a big factor in helping her get through. The bond she has with her family and close friends has helped put her, and keep her, on a path that she wants to take. Billie has learnt in recent years to be true to herself, to make the choices she wants and to do things because they feel right for her. She admits to learning from her mistakes and says that she doesn't want to be protected from failing. At the same time, she has moved past the stage of worrying about what others think about her.

Billie has deliberately stepped away from using social media too much as she became aware that it can fuel negative emotions. Billie has said that she tries hard to stay off her phone and only posts when she feels comfortable doing so or when she needs to get a message out there. When she was much younger, dance was another method of boosting her mental health. The freedom to move and express herself helped to clear her mind and release the thoughts that were upsetting her.

"The most important thing right now would probably be maintaining my happiness [...] I want to stay happy – that's a big goal for me."

Billie speaking to
Vanity Fair in 2019

"I'm living in this moment, but I'm just not afraid of change."

Vevo LIFT interview, 2018

"I don't wanna make money if it means being someone I don't want to be."

Vevo LIFT interview, 2018

"The internet put me in a really bad mood and I just was like, 'I don't need this in my life.'"

OMR Podcast, 2019

"Success is not how well people know you, it's how you're looked at."

Vanity Fair, 2019

AWESOME EILISH INFO

Billie loves spiders and used to have a pet tarantula. In her video for 'You Should See Me In A Crown', several spiders crawl all over her, with one even coming out of her mouth. Eek!

A fan once gave Billie a huge stuffed Blohsh made from soft material. She loved it so much that she slept with it for weeks.

It's unusual for a teenager, but Billie admits to enjoying cleaning and tidying her bedroom and making her bed each day.

Billie doesn't enjoy smiling and it's very rare for her to smile in a photograph.

If Billie could choose any superhero power, it would be to fly. She'd also like to be able to choose when to be famous and when not to be famous.

Billie now has a stack of celebrity pals and revealed that the most famous people in her phone's contacts are Justin Bieber, Ariana Grande and Drake.

Billie loves eating frozen pineapple that has been microwaved. It sounds awful, but it's a tasty treat for her!

In a video Billie created of her buying trainers, she spent over £1,800 on three classic pairs of Nike shoes.

Billie is a huge animal lover. She says her favourite animal is a horse but she's really fond of dogs as well.

Some of Billie's favourite foods are mashed potato, tofu, burritos and tortilla chips with guacamole dip.

Billie's favourite film of all time is *Fruitvale Station*, which is a hard-hitting biographical drama set in California.

While Billie mainly expresses herself through her music and fashion choices, she is also vocal about worldwide issues that she believes are important.

Billie acknowledges that she's often held up as a role model. Although not always comfortable with this status, the platform Billie has gives her a chance to speak out and express opinions on a range of worthwhile matters. From the benefits of being vegan and protecting the environment to animal rights, social inequality and politics, there are many topics that Billie feels passionate about.

BEING VEGAN

Billie is a vegan, which means that she does not consume any food or drink that's come from animals or use products made from animals. Her parents raised her as a vegetarian and Billie is proud that she has never eaten meat. When she was around 13, she made the decision to become vegan and posted a strong message about her choice: "I love animals and I just think there's no point in creating something out of an animal when the animal is already there. Leave animals alone." Billie doesn't 'mouth off' at meat eaters and would never be the preachy sort, but she will promote the benefits of a plant-based diet – she even admitted how it has improved her skin.

PROTECTING THE ENVIRONMENT

"Up to one million species are becoming extinct because of mankind's actions, and time is running out." That's the blunt message Billie gave during a climate crisis video for the environmental organization Greenpeace. Billie is determined to spread her environmental message through YouTube clips, interviews and her social media channels. Billie hails the pioneering young activist Greta Thunberg for the change in attitudes she has helped inspire and believes that we all need to do more to reduce plastic pollution and emissions.

"OUR EARTH IS WARMING UP AND OUR OCEANS ARE RISING. EXTREME WEATHER IS WRECKING MILLIONS OF LIVES."

Billie, Greenpeace video, 2019

EQUALITY FOR WOMEN

Accepting the Billboard Woman of the Year Award in December 2019 gave Billie a platform to express her views on equality and female pioneers. "I want to thank all the women in the past who have been the reason I can be the way that I am and do what I want, and like paved the way for me and inspired an entire generation of young women," she declared during her emotional speech. She acknowledges that she dresses in a particular way because she doesn't want to be defined by her body shape, but equally believes that women should feel able to wear whatever they want to.

DID YOU KNOW?

When Billie was planning her 'Where Do We Go?' tour, she wanted it to be as green as possible. No plastic straws would be allowed and fans would be asked to bring their own water bottles.

POLITICAL POWER

When Billie turned 18 in December 2019, she was proud that it meant she could finally vote in her country. Ahead of the Super Tuesday elections the following March, she posted a Twitter video saying: "Like a lot of you I am going to be voting for the first time, and so are you. You've got to make sure you're registered to vote already ... do it." Urging people, especially teens and young adults, to have their say is an important message that resonates around the world. Billie's strong views on environmental issues have prompted her to insist that young people's votes are just as important as those of older generations – because her age group has to live with the consequences of harmful decisions and damage to the planet.

DRUG FREE

Billie is content that she has never taken recreational drugs in her life. Speaking to The Guardian aged 17, she said: "I've never got high; I've never smoked anything in my life ... It's just not interesting to me." Many famous artists have fallen into problems with substance abuse, but thankfully Billie is sending a clear message to her fans about its perils. She has already lost people she knew because of drug addictions, and her anti-drug views extend to never drinking alcohol or smoking cigarettes. Billie acknowledges that she's no angel. However, when it comes to chemical dependencies she stays well clear. Her attitude sends a positive message to society in general.

ROLE MODEL

It's often difficult for adults to cope with the pressure of being a role model, so you can imagine how hard it is for Billie as a teenager. Billie hasn't shot to fame off the back of one viral hit or a YouTube video explosion – instead she's had to grow up in the public eye. "I completely recognize the responsibility and I do think about it,

BILLIE'S STRONG VIEWS ON ENVIRONMENTAL ISSUES HAVE PROMPTED HER TO SAY THAT YOUNG PEOPLE'S VOTES ARE JUST AS IMPORTANT AS THOSE OF OLDER GENERATIONS.

but it's not going to change the way that I am," she told The New York Times at the age of 17. She protects herself to a degree by not sharing everything she does on social media and has learnt to think before she posts. She may use swear words in interviews, but interestingly the whole of her debut studio album is free from bad language, which was a decision that she and Finneas made together.

BEING YOURSELF

Billie's individualism makes her stand out from the crowd and she will always encourage people to express themselves and be real. When internet rumours spread about a condition she has called Tourette Syndrome, which causes a person to have involuntary movements called tics, Billie spoke out. "Everybody in my family, all my friends and the people that are closest to me know that I have it and it's not anything different. I also learned that a lot of my fans have it, which made me feel more at home by saying it," she explained on The Ellen Show.

FAN-TASTIC!

Billie has millions of fans all around the world. While celebrities like Dua Lipa, James Corden, Sam Smith and Taylor Swift are big admirers, the majority of Billie's fans and followers are people just like you – people who stream her music and watch her videos all of the time.

"I want to be as reachable as I can for them, as equal ... we're all on the same level and we are all the same age! Even the idea of paid meet and greets, I don't like that idea because that automatically puts me on a different level and I don't want that."

Billie speaking to KROQ-FM, 2018

During her first tours in 2017 and early 2018, Billie was able to – and happy to – go into the crowds and mingle with her fans after the shows. She would pose for pictures and make her supporters' dreams come true. This shows how connected the artist wants to be with the people who pay to come to her performances and stream her content. Sadly, she is now such a global star that entering into the crowds like that isn't possible, but she retains that passion for pleasing her audiences. In February 2020, Billie made an appearance on Capital FM in London, surprising a 16-year-old superfan who acts as a carer for their mum and brother. It was Billie's small way of giving something back to this young fan who sacrifices so much for their family.

DID YOU KNOW?

There's debate over what Billie's fans should be known as. Some call themselves 'Avocados' after Billie's previous Instagram handle (@wherearetheavocados), but others like to be called 'Eyelashes' or 'Pirates'.

THINGS THAT PROVE
YOU'RE A BILLIE FAN ...

ROCKING THE MERCH

Billie's official clothing wear is simple and slick and in early 2020 it offered tops, hats and jewellery with her Blohsh symbol on. Wearing gear inspired by Billie shows that you're dedicated to the cause and want to look just like the talented teen.

ACTING LIKE BILLIE

You don't need to jet across the world on tour and hit up billions of streams to be like Billie. If you treat others well, inspire yourself to be the best that you can and work hard for your dreams, then you're channelling Billie's awesome ethos and beliefs.

SINGING AT CONCERTS

She LOVES it when the fans sing along with her and bounce around to top tunes such as 'Bad Guy'. Billie has commented that it's great to hear the different accents of her fans too, from Australia to New Zealand and France to England.

ENJOYING THIS BOOK

You're reading this book and loving the info, facts, stories and pictures in it, so that proves you're a total fan. Make sure you take the quiz at the end (pages 58–59) to test your superfan status.

"It's really special for me. I don't like to call them my fans because they're my family; they're the only reason I'm anything."
Billie speaking in 2017 to *Harper's Bazaar*

"... even other kids wearing merch with my name on it, that come to my show – they're like homies. I genuinely feel like I'm seeing my friends again."
Billie speaking in 2019 to *Variety*

"I want to be the artist that I wanted to be a fan of!"
Billie speaking in 2019 to MTV Australia

"The only reason you're there is because of them."
Billie speaking in 2018 to *Access*

"I make what I make because I wanna make it, and the fact that other people love that is incredible to me."
Billie speaking in 2018 to *Access*

CONCERTS, TOURING & FESTIVALS

The numbers connected to Billie's tours and concerts are simply incredible. When her 2020 global 'Where Do We Go?' tour was first announced, the venues sold out within days and the 42-date extravaganza was soon extended to 60 appearances. In fact, Billie sold 500,000 tickets within the first hour of release! Billie often says that she enjoys making "crazy shows" for the fans and that touring is one of the best parts of her job.

> "As much as my shows are for everybody else, they are also for me. It is my happy place and it is my peace and joy."
>
> Billie speaking in 2019 to the Zach Sang Show

But touring wasn't always a happy experience for her. On her early tours, such as the 'Don't Smile At Me' tour in 2017 and 'Where's My Mind' tour in 2018, she was often quite unhappy. "The first couple of tours that I did were just like agonizingly horrible. I was overworked, I wasn't sleeping, I wasn't eating enough ... it was like dreadful," she said on the OMR Podcast in 2019. The team around Billie has learnt to create a tour schedule that suits Billie and Finneas, and allows her to have fun and something close to a normal life along the way.

When she was 15 and 16, the venues Billie performed in were small theatres and arts centres, catering for hundreds rather than thousands of fans each night. This allowed her to grow comfortable with performing. Billie could easily have sold out larger arenas even at that age, but she took the decision to carefully learn her craft and grow year on year. It's quite easy to search YouTube from a few years ago and discover videos from fans who are within touching distance of Billie at her concerts. These days that just wouldn't be possible, even though she still likes to get as close as she can to the crowds.

COACHELLA, 2019

California's Coachella is one of the most iconic gigs in North America, and Billie's debut appearance stunned fans. Opening with 'Bad Guy', she controlled the lively crowd and provided powerful performances of songs such as 'You Should See Me In A Crown', 'Bury A Friend' and 'All The Good Girls Go To Hell'. Accompanied by Finneas and a drummer, she coped amazingly with the pressure of being on one of the most famous stages in the world.

GLASTONBURY, 2019

Billie had performed in the UK before this appearance, with her 'Where's My Mind' tour starting in London in 2018, but Glastonbury became her showpiece set in Britain. Strutting on the Other Stage at the legendary festival with several thousand looking on, her tunes and ballads rocked the sun-drenched audience. 'Bad Guy', 'Ocean Eyes', 'Xanny', 'Copycat' and other well-known songs struck a real chord with the huge crowd. Billie will one day return to Glasto as the headline act, that's for sure!

> "I'm unhappy doing this without the people that I love. I've also always been the kind of person that needs a group of people with me all the time."
>
> Billie speaking in 2019 to the Zach Sang Show

DID YOU KNOW?

Billie says that the downside of going on tour is missing her friends in California. Her mum, dad and brother tour with her, however.

Billie is a very visual artist. This means that she works hard at not only the way her content sounds but also the way it looks – from her style and actions on stage to the direction and details in her videos. Having the condition synesthesia, which means that her senses are interconnected, has exacerbated this and has also led to Billie creating so many wonderful visual interpretations of her songs. She has a huge input in her videos and directs and edits many of them.

"Visuals are so important to me, and I'm so proud to be in a place where I can present my creative vision exactly as I want it. Thank you to everyone who has put their trust in me."

Billie speaking in 2019 about the video for 'Xanny'

For many artists, making music videos is a tedious chore, full of endless takes, singing and standing in front of magic green screens. This can be the case for Billie, but she also always has the end goal in sight and understands the importance of a powerful video in a digital world.

DID YOU KNOW?

Billie is really keen on directing a movie in the future. She thinks that the 2011 film *We Need To Talk About Kevin*, by the Scottish director Lynne Ramsay, is beautifully shot and she aspires to create a piece of work to that high standard.

> ## "... well, how am I supposed to get the job if I can't get any experience?"

'XANNY'

The video to 'Xanny' was the first that Billie directed herself. At the end of 2019, Billie spoke at length to *The Guardian* about her passion for being behind the camera as well as in front of it. "Since the beginning of my career I wanted to direct videos. I told everybody that immediately and they were like, 'well, you don't have any experience and you don't have the time'," she explained. "There's this weird world of 'you don't have any experience so you can't have the job'. It's like, well, how am I supposed to get the job if I can't get any experience? I think that's a big problem in the world with women. I don't think people like us being the boss, especially because I was 13, 14, 15 years old. They really didn't want a 14-year-old to direct a music video. But I knew I wanted to and I convinced them, I got their trust, and from here on I want to do my own videos."

Billie admits that 'Xanny' is a song that makes you feel uncomfortable. It's about an experience she had of her friends drinking and smoking around her, which she was very unhappy with. "It feels like a headache ... the verses are like what smoke looks like and the choruses are what it feels like," she said to YouTube Music. The video is simple, using one setting of Billie dressed in pale clothes against a pale background. Smoke is blown into her face and cigarettes are painfully extinguished on her. Billie has an expression-less look on camera but it's still an emotional video – she leaves the video for the final minute as smoke continues to blow in and eventually the screen fades to black. It's powerful and very meaningful to Billie as her debut directed video.

'EVERYTHING I WANTED'

The video for this song was the second that Billie directed (after 'Xanny'). The song is about her love for Finneas and how he is the one person she can always trust and rely on. The video begins serenely with Billie driving through a city and with Finneas in the passenger seat, but then takes a dark twist as she drives into the ocean and the car sinks and fills with water. The most poignant part of the four minutes and 40 seconds feature is when Finneas puts out his hand and Billie takes hold of it as the water level rises. The brother and sister even smile at each other, which is quite unusual for Billie to do! Just like 'Xanny', the end credit on screen reads 'Directed by Billie Eilish' – she is clearly proud to let her fans know that she was the video's creative force.

DID YOU KNOW?

The line "but my head was under water" from 'Everything I Wanted' was actually recorded with Billie's mouth underwater.

'WHEN THE PARTY'S OVER'

"What video am I most proud of? 'When The Party's Over'. It came out exactly the way I wanted it to come out. I had a vision in my head, we worked really hard on it, we did a bunch of takes and then we got it." That's what Billie revealed to *Teen Vogue* about another of her most famous videos. Billie didn't direct this one, but had the idea for the striking image of black tears rolling down her cheeks, set against her contrasting white outfit. With over 480 million YouTube views within 18 months of its release, it's proved to be another smash hit with her fans. Like 'Xanny', the video is simple, powerful and pure with the haunting ballad perfectly in sync with the disturbing single-shot feature.

DID YOU KNOW?

Billie had to record the part of the video where black liquid runs down her face six times in total.

'YOU SHOULD SEE ME IN A CROWN'

Speaking to Amazon Music, Billie said: "I don't know why 'You Should See Me In A Crown' was the idea for the spider thing, but I just loved the idea of doing the one thing that people would be like, 'urgh!' I had this idea where I wanted to look at the camera, open my mouth and have a spider crawl out." What Billie described is the most memorable part of this video, which features lots of spiders crawling all over her white baggy costume. If you really don't like these creepy-crawlies, then this vid isn't for you!

'BAD GUY'

As Billie's most popular video, pulling in around 800 million views within its first year, 'Bad Guy' was edited by the artist, which meant she had a say in how the different scenes flowed and were cut together in production. Nine different stories and settings are interwoven through the video, ranging from Billie in a white shirt looking at the camera with a bloodied nose, to riding a toy car and wearing a diving snorkel. The theme of 'Bad Guy' is how Billie can act fake and be a tough guy too, if she wants, and mocking those who also act that way. The video is dark and weird in places – especially the final scene – but also fun and frivolous.

TIME-OUT TIMELINE

2015

2016

2017

Billie begins making waves in the music industry and signs to Darkroom, a division of the Interscope label.

She records a video for 'Ocean Eyes' and the song is released on the US Hot 100 list, going on to spend 20 weeks on the chart and eventually peak at number 84.

Her songs and performances grow in popularity on digital platforms. For the Sofar Sounds YouTube Channel, she performs her new song 'Six Feet Under'. It receives its first hearing on Apple Music's Beats 1 show.

This becomes a huge year for the artist. 'Bellyache', which would go on to become a double platinum hit, is her first big video smash on YouTube, pulling in over 360 million views over the next three years.

'Bored', 'Watched' and 'Copycat' also get their first releases to her fans, with much acclaim for her individual style.

Her debut extended play (EP) album comes out. Called *Don't Smile At Me*, it reaches number 14 on the US charts and similar slots in other charts around the world. The collection of songs includes her hits 'Ocean Eyes' and 'Bellyache'.

She continues making appearances outside of North America, including amazing, intimate gigs in London and Berlin to lucky fans.

In September 2017, Apple Music names Billie as their 'Up Next' artist and make a short documentary about her. She is thrilled to be branded as an exciting emerging talent.

In November, Billie Eilish and her older brother, Finneas O'Connell, release the song 'Ocean Eyes' on SoundCloud, sung by Billie and written by Finneas. It introduces the world to the teenager's fabulous talent – she's still just 13!

Within days the song is listened to thousands of times, which the siblings are not expecting at all.

It has been an amazing career so far for the world's hottest musical talent!

2018 2019 2020

2018

Billie's biggest tour so far, called 'Where's My Mind', kicks off in February and includes 26 dates around Europe and America. England, France, Italy, Germany and Sweden are taken in before a range of appearances back in the US.

'Lovely', a touching collaboration with Khalid, provides her highest US chart slot of number 64, as well as her first entry into the UK singles scene, reaching number 47.

'You Should See Me In A Crown' climbs even higher in the US, peaking at number 41, and 'When The Party's Over' shoots to 29 as both sides of the Atlantic are now well versed in Billie's incredible style and voice. The latter takes her inside the UK chart's top 30 for the first time, reaching number 21.

2020

Billie collects five Grammy Awards in January. She is the youngest artist ever, and first woman, to scoop the four principle prizes of Best New Artist, Record of the Year, Song of the Year and Album of the Year. Finneas wins Producer of the Year.

In February, she releases her theme tune to the upcoming James Bond film. 'No Time To Die' gives Billie her first UK number-one song and she is the youngest artist in history to record a theme song for the famous film franchise.

Billie wins her first Brit Award in February, after being named Best International Female Solo Artist.

2019

The teenager's Spotify stream count tops 1 billion in January.

Billie scores her first top ten UK hit in February when 'Bury A Friend' rises to number six. It goes on to spend 21 weeks in total in Britain's top 100 list.

At the end of March, her first studio album, *When We All Fall Asleep, Where Do We Go?*, finally drops. She becomes the first performer born in the 2000s to top the US album charts, and the youngest woman in UK chart album history to take the top spot.

In total, 14 of the album's songs chart at the same time in the US's Hot 100, another record for a female artist.

The song 'Bad Guy', taken from the album, also gives Billie her debut number-one hit in the US. The track reaches number two in the UK and spends 49 weeks in total on the chart.

When We All Fall Asleep, Where Do We Go? finishes as Spotify's most-streamed album of the year as her total streams tick past 6 billion.

BILLIE BRAIN TEASERS

Now that you're a superfan, it's time to take this brilliant Billie quiz packed with fun questions all about your musical hero. Write down your answers, and then turn to page 60 to see how you did. Good luck!

1. When was Billie born? Was it 25th December, 2000, 18th December, 2001 or 1st December, 2002?

....

2. Which of these is one of Billie's actual middle names: Bunny, Phoenix or Pirate?

....

3. With which singer did she record the song 'Lovely'?

....

4. What's the title of her first studio album?

....

5. Which song gave Billie her first number-one single in the UK charts?

....

6. What did Billie nickname her first car? Was is 'the Dragon', 'the Beast' or 'the Boss'?

....

7. Which of these British groups heavily influenced her as a child: Radiohead, Oasis or The Beatles?

....

8. Which artist was Billie obsessed with when she was growing up, even having posters of them on her bedroom walls?

....

9. What's the name of her official logo? Is it 'Finneas', 'Janky' or 'Blohsh'?

....

10. The video to which song was the first that she directed herself?

....

11. What streaming service does she credit as helping to launch her career in 2015?

....

12. Which fruit used to be included in part of her official Instagram handle?

....

13. What's her favourite brand of sports shoes? Is it Adidas, New Balance or Nike?

....

14. Which song gave Billie her first number-one single in the US charts?

....

15. What word completes this Billie Eilish song title: 'Bury A ...'?

....

16. What is her brother's surname (and Billie's real surname)?

....

17. What creatures famously feature in the video to 'You Should See Me In A Crown'?

....

18. What's the name of the huge Californian festival that Billie
played for the first time in spring 2019?

....

19. Which of these instruments does Billie not play: the ukulele, piano or trumpet?

....

20. At what age has Billie said she first coloured her hair purple?

....

So, what does the future hold for Billie Eilish? In the last few years she has grown from being a bedroom pop star to the biggest entertainer in the world, all before she turned 18. She has earned a stash of cash, has fans across the globe and artists are queuing up to work with her. One thing is for sure, though – Billie will keep growing, changing and surprising her audiences.

"It's a big commitment to be Billie Eilish! I am what's inspiring me to be better ... everything I am doing makes me want to do more."

Billie speaking to the OMR Podcast in 2019

In a fun and candid way, she has begun to talk about how she feels now that she's reaching the end of her teenage years. She has questioned whether people will still be interested in her when she's no longer 'young', suggesting that her tender age was perhaps one of her endearing qualities. In reply, her fans will undoubtedly be happy to grow older and mature alongside her, taking in her creative twists and turns along the way. Clearly all artists have to change and if Billie does move further into fashion or making movies, the crowds will still come and the attention on her will still be huge.

"I'm not going to tell myself to do something different next year – I'm just going to do what I want next year."

Billie speaking to *Vanity Fair* in 2019

Billie's attitude to working with other artists may change over time, too. As a teen, she has been happy to solely write and perform with Finneas, with the very occasional collaboration with other high-profile artists. These collaborations excite her fans but are not something they crave, as Billie's skill is in making the most of what her individual talents have to offer. She will keep directing and editing her own music videos too, now that 'Xanny' and 'Everything I Wanted' have proved her class behind the camera. This book began by saying that Billie is an artist like no other, and that will still be true one year, two years or ten years from now.

Thank you, Billie ... we love you!

BILLIE BRAIN TEASERS

– ANSWERS:

1. 18th December, 2001
2. Pirate
3. Khalid
4. *When We All Fall Asleep, Where Do We Go?*
5. 'No Time To Die'
6. The Dragon
7. The Beatles
8. Justin Bieber
9. Blohsh
10. 'Xanny'
11. SoundCloud
12. Avocado
13. Nike
14. 'Bad Guy'
15. Friend
16. O'Connell
17. Spiders
18. Coachella
19. Trumpet
20. Nine

BONUS QUESTION

On the front cover of this book, there's a soundwave. Can you guess what it represents?

Answer: A soundwave of a voice saying "Billie Eilish".